The Virgin Formica

The Virgin Formica

Sharon Mesmer

Hanging Loose Press
Brooklyn, New York

Published by Hanging Loose Press, 231 Wyckoff Street, Brooklyn,
NY, 11217. All rights reserved. No part of this book may be
reproduced without the publisher's written permission, except for
brief quotations in reviews.

Printed in the United States of America

10 9 8 7 6 5 4 3 2 1

Hanging Loose Press thanks the Literature Program of the New
York State Council on the Arts for a grant in support of the
publication of this book.

Cover design by David Borchart and Sharon Mesmer

Library of Congress Cataloging-in-Publication Data

Mesmer, Sharon
   The virgin formica / Sharon Mesmer.
      p. cm.
   Poems.
   ISBN-13: 978-1-931236-91-1 (pbk.)
   ISBN-13: 978-1-931236-92-8 (cloth)
   I. Title.
   PS3563.E74628V57 2008
   811'.54--dc22

                                          2007047323

Produced at The Print Center, Inc. 225 Varick St.,
New York, NY 10014, a non-profit facility for liter-
ary and arts-related publications. (212) 206-8465

Table of Contents

III. The Virgin Formica

To David Borchart, as always,
and in memory of Lydia Tomkiw, Jacqui Disler
and Yllka Domi

In the Spiritual History Office

Canticle

Thank you for asking me to submit to your magazine,
Dead Fluffy Coyote,
but I haven't been writing much poetry lately.
I've been rockin'.
Or, I should say, rockin' *again*.
Because I used to rock.
I started rockin' at the age of ten,
me and my sister sitting with Dad in the Rambler,
watching the planes take off and land.
In fact, that's where I first rocked:
in that Rambler, with a transistor radio pressed to my ear.
And I rocked for a long time.
A pretty long fuckin' time!
But then *somebody* came along and made me self-conscious about
      rockin'.
Somebody said my rockin' was "anti-intellectual."
They said I'd never get a tenure-track job teaching creative writing at
      a university
if I didn't stop rockin'.
So I stopped rockin'.
What was I thinking?
Didn't I understand that, yes,
the heavy bombardment was a hellish environment
but also the natural condition of creation?
Oh, you brilliant neurotics, syphilitics, and hyperpriapic lead
      guitarists — you knew.
Proust knew in his cork-lined room
that rockin' arises afresh daily from every afflicted attitude,
and even *not* rockin'
forms a bridge between forgotten continents.
I may have epilepsy, brain atrophy, "milk leg," bottleflies infesting
      my eyes,

and the belief that my legs and arms are angry clowns,
but I'm rockin' like a cross between Anna Akhmatova and Dolly Parton,
like broken post-Bolshevik teacups and flea markets.
Oh, too late came I to love you,
rockin' so ancient and so new!
Oh Lucifer, light-bringer,
singer of our hymns to failure,
cut us loose from our tribal pieties,
our forebodings at what this new age means,
for we shall be known by new names.
And if our decency is fatigued
let us eat its meat with similar spoons.
Who knows the secrets of the universe,
whether Marilyn Monroe had eleven toes?
Rockin' knows.
Like the bone at the beginning of *2001*,
what befell the beginning keeps befalling,
and something old and mostly forgotten
can rock the marginalized fifty million.
We're always being asked to do the impossible,
and so now I'm asking you to rock.
I'm *begging* you to rock.
I have no doubts about your faults.
But your faults give birth to a dancing star.
Sure, harsh carcasses are crisscrossing the pit,
souls fluttering up the rotunda like confetti
but joy lurks there.
I know 'cause I've been there.
It's hard to get back what's been forgotten.
But it's easy to start rockin'.

Just This

It came to me
suddenly —
Three Dog Night
were really great!
And the revelation
engendered a seizure
that revealed
the ephemereality
of eternity:
how Theseus in the labyrinth
is everyone's predicament,
how the milk of three ornery daughters
spawned irony,
and how every morning
trails clouds of glory.
But it was after midnight
that things got interesting
in the low-ceilinged kitchen,
with the slop sink sweating,
and the door to the back garden open,
and us the only ones on the block
still awake.
The next day
a powerful wind
whipped through Yankee Stadium —
I saw it happen on television —
and eight minutes later
it arrived in Brooklyn
to disturb the birds
nesting in the air conditioner:
proof that everything
is always beginning and becoming.
To bring it into being

means always deploying.
Because the portal
to the river of cordial
closed in 1960,
reducing me
and all who came after me
to a cowboy vulgarity,
to fluidity
on a wave of dissipation,
but thus a deeper appreciation
for the play of changing
light and shadow
on a window fan on a rainy day,
and the certainty
that the light we imagine we see
with eyes half closed,
squinting into trees,
is the most beautiful
anyone's ever seen.

I believe I should like
to decorate your life
with a painted scale model
of the Apollo 11 lunar module,
and then bow out
in a blaze of italics,
anxious for exit,
yet anxious to persist.
And so I'll go
erase the notes for this poem,
so that you'll believe
it came to me
on its own
as just this.

My Juice

I'm holding my juice,
holding my cleanliness,
I'm holding my juice in my cleanliness
    with my spiders
        my release
        my virginity
        and forgiveness.
I'm covering you with love
in the guise of my juice,
while cowering in the face
of so much confusion.
My cleanlinesss becomes a contusion,
and now I'm withholding my juice,
withholding my contusion,
I'm withholding my juice in my contusion
    with my starlight
        my dark ages
        my dust ruffles and Bibles
        and vicious bird foibles
           in my crawlspace.
In the absence of juice, a crowd of consorts
stinks up my crawlspace
and I feel my way blindly
toward the Holy of Holies:
an old plastic bag wound 'round a branch
torn and tattered like an old coccoon
where I receive communion
in the form of my juice.
And now I'm upholding my juice,
upholding my communion,
upholding my juice in my communion,
avoiding the brightly lit palaces
for the twilit interstices

between Venus and Lucifer
in the coalescence of debris
           that made the moon
to touch with my most febrile feeler
my most precious and at the same time insecure
possession.

Never Lose Your Sense of Wonder

I

There's a fawn on the lawn
and it's ruining our weekend.
Will its mother ever come?
Or will we have to care for it in a nursing home?
Out here on Sparrow Lane there are no sparrows,
and everything's the opposite of Brooklyn:
blue jays are timid,
mourning doves duke it out with robins on the ground,
and a titmouse hops into a hole with a junco.
Can we call the cops on those crows?
I want to say to a waitress, "Hi, I'd like lunch,"
but there is no waitress, just the crash and burn
of anticipation onto quietude
and birdsongs like drops of water.
Now I want Indian food,
the chance to juice a forsaken grapefruit.
Ah, how this anxiety might subside
in the quiet contemplation of a lake.
They say the sun is a good source of vitamin D,
never mind the skin cancer.
But I prefer my indoor pallor,
my solitary ruminations on art as a sentient entity
(despite a whole forest of sentience surrounding me),
and how my fingers look and act different when I wear nail polish.
More delicate-like.

II

In the city, here's how I think:
if I can close the window before the jackhammer starts,

everything will be alright.
If I can smell the lilacs on the bush in front of the house
before I close the window
before the jackhammer starts,
everything will be alright.
If the lilacs aren't dead yet, and I can smell them
before I close the window before the jackhammer starts,
then everything will be alright.
Out here in the country my thoughts spiral, too;
the difference is, they don't come back.
They just keep going, with no echo.
Things like:
Hammer and sick
A sorry dulcimer
The flesh variations
But that's about it:
just a list of non sequiturs which, as we know,
is already a poem.
To hear one's name spoken in a revolving door
when one is going through it alone
is one of the city's great mysteries.
But what does it mean?
It doesn't matter; you'll never know.
"They" can't tell you anything directly;
the rule is, you have to ask,
and that means knowing the questions.
Like: *Is navigation by magnetism possible?* for example.
Or: Why did Springsteen turn out to not *be the future of rock and roll?*
Well, it's a beginning,
a way of hearing Hope talking.
Or maybe listening.

III

I love the smell of wood smoke in summer,
a dewpoint trembling a full spectrum of color.

But I miss sideshows by seashores,
suppers with vulgar bankers,
my coveted, blue-collar dollars.
I'm here because sometimes the city streets expect too much of me.
I can't fulfill the promise of the bright avenues.
Oh, Mystery, why can't I be three people pounding rice,
a surprise of butterflies,
wealthy?
My guru says I gave up a vast inheritance in Eternity
for the ability to write poetry.
All I know is, if I start drinking now,
I'll be unconscious by Christmas.
And speaking of drinking, I need tea.
Chinese tea, from the last century,
in a warm, rinsed teapot.
Oh, is that too "consumer" for you?
I say to some critical, invisible ex-lover.
Okay: and to truly comprehend the beauty
of a slop sink at evening.
And — yes, yes — to tell of the triumph of a friendless girl
over the most powerful corporations.
But I'll never accomplish any of that.
I'm too concerned with comfort,
too attached to order.
I hated arriving in all those foreign places with nowhere to stay.
Even in dreams I obsessively clean.

IV

The sound of the knife in the mayonnaise jar
as we sit down at the table to play Scrabble
speaks of neither Indian food nor tea,
but of a more fitting end to our day in the country.
The self-help people tell us we must
stay in rapport with source energy,
practice radical humility,

and never lose our sense of wonder.
My days of playing to the absinthe tent may be ended,
but I can still marvel at the hourglass at the edge of the forest,
sing the praises of earthenware vessels passed through windows,
and pray hard and long that Fate won't go apeshit
on that poor little fawn.

Stupid University Job

Your loveliest of sway-backs;
of mine I was once ashamed,
and my uni-brow and crooked teeth,
and red hair my mother never let me wash
all winter,
afraid I'd catch a draft.
She wouldn't let me bathe, either,
which made gym class a horror.
I thought I had it bad
until I met that handsome Scottish man
whose parents tried to make him spontaneously combust
by feeding him haggis laced with gunpowder
and making him sleep in the stove.
Instead of an ear, he had a shiny, snail-shaped ridge.
I guess we all have our tragic flaw.
Mine is like that of the naked man
who holds up a sign that says "I'm naked"
and runs screaming through the park.
My handlers say I'm difficult,
but don't you believe it.
My soul still radiates a luminous intensity
despite this stupid university job.

Brenda Coultas's Coat

Like a crazy pony
or a mod giraffe,
on the back of her chair at the reading,
and her shirt of lionesses and impala —
or kudu? are they kudu? —
and her Jo Malone cologne . . .
and now I've lost the thread of Lee Ann's reading
(something about . . . breast feeding?)
and I've just kicked over my wine
("Do you want me to hold that?" Edwin had asked,
 and I should've let him)
onto my book and now it looks
like Joseph Brodsky's drooling blood,
which seems like a sign,
or portent,
or message
from the post-Bolshevik poets
to us about the coming flood
of harsh carcasses
across our event horizon, the Burgess Shale
was plagued by catastrophe,
it's a recipe for creation, really,
for vitality out of nonliving ingredients,
like lightning in a reaction vessel, history
can be such a charming chemistry . . .

oh, Brenda Coultas's coat,
on the back of her chair,
next to Eugene Ostashevsky's coat
at the reading.

Retarded Aerosmith World

Where dirt bikes meet hips
there's a smell of wood smoke and pussy
there's a windswept junkyard dog
there's nothing for a long time and then there's sex
where the twelve-point centaur rests:
> little blue trailer
> far end of the parking lot
> behind the Walgreens
where there's starlight through dimity curtains
and someone bent over a bathtub
and three people in another room
smoking on the soul cakes.
Later there's a lily bath
and a new hairdo for a funeral
and a great love torn asunder
but another love renewed.

What Becomes Us

People don't question wholesale bullshit like they used to.
People don't break into song.
People don't strike things from the record.
Nobody joins the circus.
Nobody orders Chinese takeout, opens a bottle of Chianti,
      and calls that a party.
Who chews Juicy Fruit?
Who swabs the decks of poop?
Who still believes that every great love is in some measure a terrible
      mistake?
Who still carries within a bodily frame the indelible stamp
      of lowly origins?
Do women bear stones now instead of children?
Do people still see the significance of moonlight through a frosted
      skylight airshaft window? of Vaseline on stained glass?
Do people still sit cross-legged on curbs fashioning mental movies
      of the stories of their lives?
Does anyone burn with a hard, jewel-like flame?
Does anyone let all things happen — beauty and terror alike — unto
      them?
Does anyone suddenly, in a private hour, in the middle of vacation,
      challenge the totality of existence with a figure of maternal
      endurance?
Does the sensation of an insufficient lunch still prove worthy of poetry?
Does anyone renounce their cake and eat it too?
Where are the moral hedonists?
Where is the noble purpose? the patient energy required for
      completion? the resolution undaunted by opposition?
What is the consensus nowadays on becoming a grotesque mirror
      of one's own mother?
Is the experience of puberty still an insult to any intelligent, sensitive
      person?
Is nothingness still the ultimate simplicity?

Is anyone becoming a hero or heroine of his or her own imagination?
Is laughter still the best medicine?
Are stern angels now unrequired to hear our pleas?
Why are people overlooking expulsion and retention as important
        to the alchemical process?
Why isn't anyone doing the Blue Corn Dropsy under the flower moon?
Or dancing like Spaniards with an ox?
Why aren't they fucking in the furrows?
Why aren't they celebrating the sunflower hour with a moment
        of duck blood soup?
Has anyone ever thought of embracing the rugged industrialist
        of the secretarial sciences? And if not, why not?
Does anyone ever get out of work early on a snowy day and look
        forward to going home and masturbating?
No one sees the moon then becomes the moon, and so the moon, sadly,
        becomes no one.
People don't wear plastic bags, directing traffic.
Who's giving it away on Seventh Avenue?
Hello hello — is there anybody in there?
Just nod if you can hear me.
Is there anyone at home?
Does anyone see the young, well-built excrement collector
        descending the mountain at dusk, reappearing shortly thereafter
            in a narrow street clogged by a shrine borne by boys,
                and finally gaining fame in the ranks of a family
                    of Frankish tenors and Confucian tutors?
No!
That's because no one knows to kill the Buddha when they meet the
        Buddha.
A yellow gorilla is often the voice of reason.
And who among you can correctly answer the Seventh Riddle of
        Existence: what is the nature and purpose
        of Nature and Purpose?

What It Is

"Complacencies of the peignoir" —
what the hell does that mean anyway?
I've been trying to write since seven,
and now it's noon,
and my thoughts are all fractured, coopish,
and I should take a walk,
I should leave this room,
step right out that front door
into the vast enchanted November Poconos . . .
But no.
It's these low-key pleasures keeping me inside,
the quiet rurality which fosters contemplation:
the perfection of the art vs. the perfection of the life,
something I've been pondering since I began temping,
foregoing both rapture and rhapsody
to accept the magical contradictions of syntax.
Now the toilet flushes
and David's coming downstairs.
You should never hitch your star, he sings,
to a nitro-burning funny car.
Now he's boiling water for ramen noodles,
going out to chop wood . . .

. . . and the water's boiling over,
and David's bringing in the wood,
and I can't seem to tune the radio to my favorite station,
WPCN — "the Pocono's only all Seventies station" —
which operates out of a storefront in downtown Monticello,
which I discovered a few years ago when we spent the weekend
with Sparrow and Ellen at their summer place near Monticello,
and it was really horrible.
(Two words: "miniature golf.")

And now I'm wondering what this raucous song is.
David says it sounds like King Usniewicz and the Usniewicztones,
his Pabst-fueled sidemen,
live from Detroit's Orbit Room,
and I say,
"Yes, it's got 'Usniewicz' written all over it."
Why is there not one classical music station
in the whole of the Poconos?
I desire the purity of musical architecture,
passacaglias and fugues,
something that sounds like
a seventeenth century armorial tapestry from Incan Peru.
And David's demonstrating
how a big fat person does The Twist,
and we discuss whether Chubby Checker
was really chubby;
I say no.
We do agree, however,
that Fats Domino was really fat.
But was Little Richard little?
No information is available . . .

. . . and now it's evening,
evening in the Poconos,
and David's stretched out on the couch, saying,
"I'm having a coziness overload,"
and to that I say
"You can't be too rich, too thin, or too cozy."
And there's a little white candle
in a cold black window
and an owl outside,
and so we go outside,
and I think about the sudden beauty of the words
"voir dire",
and we walk onto the bridge and lean back
as the vast and random galaxies scatter

orisons of ursas,
and delectation hits like a brick, and I think
about that small and heavy star that orbits the dog star,
and about how inside the Universal Egg there is a spiral
of perpetual motion,
and about the riddle of lipstick,
and how I did find something
important, luminous, and wonderful,
and maybe someday I'll remember
what it was.

Laid

for Charles Borkhuis

"Laid"
as in "ugly,"
as in French.
But why ugly
when outside the kitchen window
an apple tree blooms in profusion,
and inside a black cat on a red formica table
chews a daffodil?
Last night you said,
"How do the French understand our poems?
 They're just lists of non sequiturs."
At the poetry reading the door was open
to let in the breeze.
At eight o'clock it was eighty degrees.
The mighty City beckoned,
yet we remained.
We listened, our brows furrowed,
we looked like we had migraines,
we left before we had the chance
to not get invited out afterward.
The lack of light illuminated
no one scribbling in notebooks,
no one stealing anyone's lines.
Does anyone remember ordinary beauty?
Does no one honor Mnemosyne?
On another Spring day,
back in seventh grade,
Eddie Boback came up to my desk at recess to say
"Mesmer, you're so ugly!"
That was thirty years ago.
But I remember it
like it was today.

Eddie Boback's Dead

"Eddie Boback's dead,"
my mother told me.

I think heaven must be a kind of
perfectly turned-out waiting room
upstairs of a roiling good time
just within hearing

and God a kind of
Understanding
for all those listening
poised not for all he offers, but
for all that may one day
be coming.

It gets harder and harder
as we get older
to keep our true selves uncovered.
So we need to stay naked
in order to remember.

"Eddie Boback's dead,"
my mother told me,
but what she really meant was
"You're starting menopause."

Three Pietàs

for Nancy Pinchot

Michelangelo chiseled his stone
In secret, from the hidden faces of mountains.
And he set certain store by having been born poor,
Wet-nursed by a stonecutter's wife.

To him sculpture was the more noble art,
By virtue of its being difficult:
That which is forged by the sheer brute force
Of the hammering, of the taking away.

The head of the Christ of the Pietà —
The famous one, the first of three —
Is thrown back, away from the viewer:
An unbearable beauty never meant to be seen,
And Mary rendered young, purposefully,
So that nothing would detract from her tragedy.

But how charming that Michelangelo
Hid in the Basilica by night,
Carving, by lamplight,
His name into Mary's mantle-strap
Because he'd heard some workers praising
His Pietà
As the work of some other artist.

All night long he faced the dead man,
Sitting cradled, as the dead man did,
Gazing upon what was intended
To always remain secret.

Summer, Elizabeth Street

Into a green-gold tumbler of light
along the side of the church
we surged,
a scourge upon the fading strains
of the Litany to Our Lady.
Tossing red beanies
into prairie air,
we ran with eyes closed,
past RoJo's,
Patka funeral home,
and the ochre two-flat where the Rybicki family lived,
its color a refract of noon sun
into Mexico.
All colors angled out that day
into a low-grade version of eternity
that would span three green months
and end in a Rambler
in the parking lot of a department store
across from the little airport
the day before Labor Day.

And in the evenings,
there was nothing on TV
(this was before *The Partridge Family*).
And so summer —
that one summer —
was swallowed
by the cool of the Sherman Park tavern before noon,
the bra models in the Sears catalogue,
and the girls from *Scooby-Doo*.

The Awful We Party

1

Outside reasons
(i.e., I was horny)
began to assemble the arbitrary
pace of asses into a reverse order
that determined the order
of who would be doing it with whom
(i.e., student nurses and sorority girls)
in the embellished dentist's chair behind the tiki bar,
while old leftists secretly peeped through peepholes,
roasting in their own b.o.
"What is this?" the guy in the elevator said,
smelling his finger.
I wondered.

2

Okay, I was loose,
foundering even,
a drifting archipelago of estrogen and cigarettes
in the glow of the southern erotic gardens.
Okay, there were no gardens, just a vast array of sailors,
luminous in the glow of the tiki bar's
wet t-shirt contest
(okay, it was really a sonnet competition).
They called me "Auntie Intellectual,"
to which I replied, smiling,
"Democracy is the new Christianity."
The one priest in attendance evinced a grimace,
so I showed him my "Little Keith Richard."
(Okay, it was my "vibrating sailboat.")

Splendor Crowds the Periphery

When the Famous Poet
yelled at me
for bleeding on him with my
skinned knee

and I yelled, "Yeah, well
maybe you haven't bled enough,"
you said,
"That's the stuff
  obscurity's made of."

The Solitary Mage

for Jacqui Disler

I can't say how many times
I've overstepped the limits of my age.
But these things that I know, I know,
and they writhe and shine, glitter and twist,
these feelings surge and soar,
seethe and roar.
Isn't it magnificent to have gotten this far
with no shred of hope
(but none of fear, either)?
Though I remain flayed with chains,
my own ruins overtaking me,
my soul and mind fly
past every petty weakness,
until every phase of nakedness
is plumed thoroughly with old vanities,
and my tiniest nerves vibrate
like finely drawn hair.
Only happiness can ruin this music.
But still the hours grow old quickly around me.
They whittle this wooden body,
until the horizon is but a rude streak
and daylight burns with its vulgar call.
But still and all,
no one falls.
No one ever falls.

In the Spiritual History Office

"What about a clockwork of Newtonian determinism
which sits in the world of certainty and objective reality
and creates the appearance of uncertainty and subjectivity
to our imperfect senses and inadequate measuring apparatus?"

Calude & Meyerstein, "Is the Universe Lawful?"

I

Who is the patron saint
of getting out of jury duty?
Who should I do a novena to?

And why are my erasers
drying out so fast?
It is because my desk
is too close to the stove?

II

I was really dreading
doing that book review
but as soon as I started it
the revelations began:
as I scanned the perimeters
of each poem for infractions,
I suddenly felt relieved of the need
to join the merry parry,
which seemed to require more *cojones*
than I imagined could exist
in all parts of the universe at all times
expanding and verifying
and installing and importing

36

and diving off particular points
of the gospels of Christ, into
the engulfing and fulgent radiance
of three copies of Kafka
(different translations)
in tatters atop a black baby grand
glossed with various moistures
from the subtle fluctuations
of cowboy emotions
transmitted by radio waves
and fry pan emissions.

III

Just because the sphere
is unlinear
does not mean it's also not time-bound.
Thus I began looking at things
through the eyes of all beings.
Satisfied, I ran my hand along
forgotten fences
for one last chance
at a chaste glance
off happiness.

In Damp Weather Everything Conducts

Instead of walking on the street
Which was dangerous
I walked through the arcades
Which was more dangerous
But more interesting:
The old-fashioned candy stores
Run by small, secretive men
And all the different drugstores
Connected by tiny, littered backyards or prairies —
I had to be careful not to step on a rusty nail
Or jagged glass
Or trip over fugitives from justice
Hiding in piles of garbage.
Soon it got to be too much
All that watching out for danger
So I decided to just walk in the street.
Under the elevated birds shit on me
And then I couldn't get the number twenty-two.
Finally I spotted the open-air carriage garage.
The dispatcher and his brother
   (also part-time fry cooks for the governor)
Offered to analyze my handwriting
While I waited for a driver.
I settled myself onto a couch
And wrote my name on a parchment block
With a beautiful ruby-colored pen.
But before they could get a look
My driver showed up —
A wiry old man
Freshly shaved and smelling of Palmolive.
As I walked away they called after me,
"Wait! You'll never know your future!"
I said it was okay.

All they could tell me was the future.
Not who I was
Or why.

Good Sleepin' Weather

Cold air
everywhere
and the impoverished edge
of anxiety
of kitchen knives
that thrive
under roofs the color
of horses' hooves.
After shopping at Zayre
we walked back to the Rambler
and dark was the screen
of the outdoor theater
where earlier they'd lowered a whore
from a helicopter.
"Man," Dad said,
"this is what you call
   good sleepin' weather."

Homestyle Favorites

A round of Brie, small in its wood crate
Blue green radicchio
Nutty nuggets
A movie

Lemons
Fennel
Tomatoes for Carla

Big navel cider
Bitter herbs and eggs
And fish, if it looks interesting
Vibrant, yummy

Rice cakes
Nice Cokes
Dinosaur eggs

Blue water
Green water
Clear apple juice

Many tomatoes
1 OJ
Mahi Mahi, if possible
Olives, French medley

Fresh blueberries (flat)
Tubers (any potency)
G milk
And everything else that looks good
Thank you
Thank you!
Home by 10:30

Lou Reed's New York

in Europe
they're much more receptive
to utility
and famous figures from disco
on skates

in America
if you keep looking for beauty
you'll get run over
by a pylon

to say nothing
of the contradictions
of butcher shops

I believe
we're here at the beginning
of the biggest change ever
and everybody
should be out
making music

I was there
at the beginning
on either side of the vinyl
and I was amazed
at the amount
of wasted
information

everything was wretched
to say the least

then God said,
"I'm gonna take film away
  but in return
  you get three new colors.
  We do it with razors
  and light animals"

and Michelangelo said
"Wow."

we used to reminisce
about how nice and clean
things were
but now what we miss
is filth.

Rebuilding the City of the Future

To the victor go the I-told-you-so's
when burly angels move in
wielding the implements of Haussmann.
They're here to halve the golden section
to determine the precise proportions of a mall,
to spout grand plans for elevations,
vault ribs and responds, and sequences of squares
arrayed according to intervals
of perfect consequences.
They're measuring the visceras
of lofty offices only they can see,
bulks of skyscrapers dependent on
sinewy ribs.
Their light, like the glow of frenetic carousels,
causes surges of vertigo in the Mohawks of Manhattan's
pink girders,
for they bring, not peace,
but swaths of rectilinear boulevards,
winding roads and straight
that mean the mortal ends of orchards.
"God is space," is how they pray,
"arcade, tympanum, and colonnade,
 and space is the true measure
 of our days."

Madame Bowery

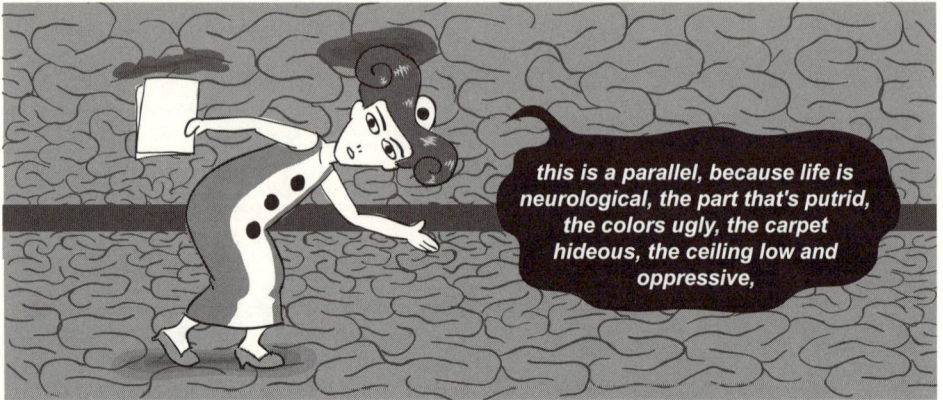

The Virgin Formica

Why You Came Back

For the jeers of the young drunks outside the Ting-A-Ling Lounge
for the dog with the chopped-off tail,
the familiar crinkle of plastic after group sex on the pool table,
. and the ensuing construction of ornamental snowmen.
For the grand cans and bad-ass mudflaps,
the local Jewish homerun king, so at home among the Eurotrash,
the warring gangs sending messages to each other via setting your
        garage on fire,
and Kenny the cab driver who always asks,
"So what are the blacks like in your neck o' the woods?"
For the cock ring displays by family members behind Lulu's little
        blue trailer,
where Ma buys her lotto, cigarettes and scandal sheets,
for the weekly dragging of the Sherman Park lagoon for a dead
        secretary,
and the official World War II civil defense flares
with which you declaim your indifference in the alley
after giving out sausage samples all day
in the meat aisle of the Certified
on your fiftieth birthday.
For the goddamn screaming children.

Blue-Collar Typeface

From the colophon to Aaron Simon's Carrier, *Insurance Editions, 2006:*
"Gotham 2003: This plain yet quintessential font was designed
by Tobias Frere-Jones and is based on vernacular architectural
lettering found throughout New York City. It is a blue-collar
typeface that is both utilitarian and perfectly simple."

Some people would like to be blue-collar
without actually having been born blue-collar.
While you,
who *were* born blue-collar,
wish you could afford something more
than the Wendy's salad bar.

Some people who are proud of how blue-collar
they think they are
speak roughly to waiters,
never look them in the eye,
and refuse to pay to get into poetry readings,
while afterwards
they're back home
putting their Manhattan co-op on the market
so they can buy a house
on the outskirts of Paris.
Some of these people are your friends.
They will surprise you.
Because someday you will discover
that all that time they seemed so interested
in what you had to say about your
blue-collar upbringing,
they never found actual blue-collar people
all that interesting.

Because a blue-collar person can't recommend them to an editor
or get them into an MFA program
or set them up with a teaching job.
Blue-collar people often don't care about
academic poetry,
the breaking of the line,
and they may not necessarily give a shit about anything
Noam Chomsky ever said.
But that doesn't mean that blue-collar people are
"utilitarian" or
"perfectly simple."
I know lots of useless,
imperfectly complicated
blue-collar people.
And their line breaks
kick your line breaks's
ass.

At Princess Olga's

The smartest of us found a coatrack;
We had linguine and peaches to protect.
First, from a rectilinear curve of earth fell Deborah,
Expellable one-hundredfold because hunchbacked.
Her form was as the moondog's,
Lunescent as Miami relatives parlaying lilaceous fake vaginas
For tape-dancing lessons.
The many Albanians were eager for tape-dancing,
Though most didn't know the first thing about dipping.
Enter the coincidental Caucasian —
Rod Praecox and his "bucketful o' muscle" —
Challenging the Albanian counterman from downstate
By one-offing Urkel with scores of sonnets each beginning:
"Even mistletoe gets the gristle."
Impeccably occluded but impotent in the afterglow,
Missy Bodybuild's side-cleaved loquacity was spent on the subject of
        groin fluency.
Number One Necromancer mercifully interrupted her:
"What do you get when you cross a Dadaist with a brooch?"
 (Answer: Aldous Huxley, who wrote with his nose.)
Meanwhile, Aggrieved Deodorant Gal unbuttoned Obese Basso's
        shirt to his navel;
His rust-colored alluvial boots begged her to.
His conceit, he said, was to meet interesting people in Nebraska,
While working as a temp for Keith Richards.
Suddenly the many Albanians began beating their women's heads
Like bongo drums.
The women stuck their tongues through their buttonholes.
Most needed water after.
Silas deployed his famous Franciscan buss as a pre-emptive measure,
Though only Aggrieved Deodorant Gal showed optimism.
The movement to dispensate any budding footpath perverts
Set off cautious offspring onto already rickety arpeggios of

"Want to make more money, Dane?
 Let hogs root through your shame."
Then, I guess, the babysitter appeared.
And maybe even a twelve-point centaur was there.
If he was anywhere.

Lonely Tylenol

It always falls most heavily
on the person least able to deal with it
falling heavily on.
In fact, it falls cats and dogs.
Like the night you walked toward me
on Eighth Street out of fog
and said you were getting married.
Life could be so pleasant,
I decided as we parted,
if each of us fucked
according to our abilities.
Two weeks later, I discovered,
Nature loses interest
after sixty-five gingersnaps up your ass,
and then your uterus falls,
followed by the broken bottleneck,
to the floor.

After they put me back together
I had scars on my tongue
and my pants were unbuttoned,
and I was nostalgic for something as simple
as your final rejection
on the bench in the square
fashioned to resemble
old Andalusia in summer.
Remember me at midnight
screaming at you from the prairie?
Because of you I got a blue jay tatoo.
It got infected.
Twice.
I know I told you
you had a beautiful cock,
but that was because I was drunk,

and we were fucking on the floor
of an empty office diamond-high
above Manhattan.
Sadly, nipples did not stand at attention.
No one spurted to kingdom come.
Rather, amid the fine cracklings of plaster
that fell from the pilasters,
you whispered,
"The elephant is in the diamond,
  and the diamond is in the lotus."
It was your winsome view of the universe.
But I was neither famous nor popular,
neither pretty nor influential.
All I could promise was to acquiesce,
like Boris Yeltsin in the Lincoln bedroom.

I had been waiting for you for so long,
waiting in the car,
waiting to lick & kiss & love you,
but when you're alone like that in your car
the car itself
can make you feel that way.
If women bought cars for sex,
like they want to,
men might start cooperating.
Anyway, my breasts were resting in your hands
like small dogs,
and my irrational desires pinnacled globally,
from the loftiest spreading tree
to the humblest Agnes Cactus.
I was like the giver of life
in the temple of the four seasons,
a nocturnal lagoon
oozing voluptuous nectars
from every diameter.
You were like a team of puppet lovers and midgets,
safe houses and teacups,
all rolled into one.

Bugs and fluids were gathering,
forming a Calgon bath in negative space.
Then came the fisting,
the clubbing,
and the flaying.
Finally, the mute twirling
and the sputtering.
"Corn?" you said, "when did I eat corn?"
What my circumstances were you knew,
you to whom the gods had given
ample appetites.
But I had a humbler station in life;
I still had a lot to earn.
"If you're lucky," you said,
"your solitary fantasies might one day transform
 one million realities."
"Anything heretofore neglected," I said
looking out at a blurry view of Jersey,
"only needs that mad housewife edge."
You called me your cross Dolores;
you were my youthless Andalusian.
I knew someday we'd be in Paris
for the lighting of the lamps.
But after that night, no more.
Nothing more.
Only long days on a mossy stained mattress
with a bee sting lingering,
and red shoes tumbling through space
in a dream.

I dread seeing you again,
on the avenue.
Every blurry view of Jersey
reminds me of you.
Is this what it means to walk naked
through the world?

For the Time Being

I

Siamese connections.
Temporal totemic unities.
The Mind finally knowing itself,
the Great Big Mind
and the Little Mind too:
that will be the Apocalyse.
At night these things come to me,
my backed-up dreams bursting forth inconveniently
like a flash flood that wrecks the doggy door.
"Seek *baaa* relief," says my demented helpmeet.
Like Bartleby I prefer not to, but I've got a good reason:
I'm a goddamn American.
And if I'm behaving badly tonight it's just because
you hauled me out here for this little talk
and the goddamn podium is made of pressboard.
The wetness of spilled drinks may occasionally
rouse me to consciousness.

II

In the beginning everything was heavier,
and nowadays even the rescuers from down under
Manhattan Bridge
have suddenly become Swedenborgian
to negotiate the vertigo of life becoming
unbearably beautiful, and then totally shitty again.
My hesitation in the vestibule
was because I'm still a bit suicidal from summer.
My thoughts move like frenzied pedestrians,
like little toads popping out of the head

of a way bigger toad.
One need not be a house to be haunted.
If a child-sized energy created the Nile,
and inspired a Japanese poet to write,
"To give birth to one poem,
 we must kill the things we love,"
the real struggle is to learn to lie supine
and remember
that bar off the boardwalk,
after the Mermaid Parade,
two big fans at the back blowing,
the jukebox playing Frank Sinata singing
"Summer Wind,"
and later,
in the Botanic Garden,
the orchids in the Temperate Pavillion.

III

The apotheosis begins
with beer drinking on the stoop
and sleeping in the breeze
from a secondhand fan.
The briefest sensation is cause for celebration:
the flash of lightning that disappears
as soon as it appears,
the long downpour,
the sound of rain on the air conditioner,
and two little girls eating baloney sandwiches
at the bottom of a long porch staircase.
Isn't it dramatic to pause and drink water?

IV

Noon.
Arabic Bride Avenue.
The sun's inexorable presence.
Despair and happiness alternating
at a dizzying clip.
Hushing the hum of all those voices can be accomplished
by something as simple as going alone to the movies.
On summer mornings, the crows,
and after a long palaver we are ready for our pleasure.
We are wretched and fabulous beyond measure.
The things we love shall become us.
All our lives, and everyone else's,
are stretched out ahead of us.
Whoever set us down in this beer garden
will soon remove us,
and send us home.

Gait Signatures

for David Amram

Enduring freedom

just turned a corner

like a picnic interloper

skilled in shindig

like a diving bird

with notes of ivory

alive within

a century of throats

like an insouciant suitor

oozing chutzpah

in vast trajectories

of tongue-tied sounds

like a soprano of the flesh

on two continents

or the monumental ice in Stuttgart's

luxurious seaport

and while Monroe enjoys

gulag maneuvers

Andean sun-worshippers plunder

Iona's etoile moguls

supplementing splendor

with parched aspects

of the sea of tranquility

like the NFL

made peevish

by female roughnecks

seeking Bowery derelicts

London rubbernecks

and gung-ho

pillows

in a wilderness of

buckwheat mush

to form the center

of an arty party's

endless source of energy

like a pagan blunderbuss

at home with a drone's

next hoax

like a star in the axle of the ear

like a nimbus portal

like a princess with a vinous touch

translating the lemming's inquiry

into stammering oriental specificity

like products of asexual reproduction

in Wisconsin

thespians

of unusually heavy youth

brainstorming the abbess

the gardener's adobe ho

and her peculiar food regimen

like an escapade of neck feathers

a case of lucky legs

a bohemian deemed seamy

in cowboy argot, and

oh, unsightly cuckoo

my impossible dream times thirteen

what happens when happiness

comes first

its negligent candor

like a zeitgeist anchored

by a famous refrain

about free agency

like sleeping pills in lieu of food

like the happy vignettes

of *That's Entertainment*

as uncertain thresholds as

gait signatures as

alternative means of transport

like eating bad food and candy

or goofing on Jimmy Durante

in ways that impose order and meaning on actions

as mundane and comforting as

washing cups at sunset

then walking alone, slowly, in the long twilight

wrapped in a blanket

in a way that apes the ancient

regularity of nature.

Flowers

after the Aztec ceremony "Flowers are Offered," from
Jerome Rothenberg's Technicians of the Sacred

The moon shines in three places when I first offer him flowers.
The moon and the evening star in a periwinkle sky like a sea of blue flowers.

A mirror stands on a table when I first offer him flowers, and people are arranging their hair in that mirror, arranging flowers. When I first offer him flowers my fingers are straight and brought together so the tips touch as in talk or song, in a dead language that means "flowers are offered." My language is also dead, so I must instead offer flowers.

I offer flowers and I sow flowers. I am the caretaker of flowers. I pick flowers and search out flowers to bring to him in the temperate dining hall of the forest. I string garlands of blue flowers like torches to light his way across the water. He is protected by a viper, so upon the water I cast a necklace of flowers, a hat, a brooch, a shield of blue flowers. I construe a perfume of threaded and stewed flowers, and I clothe myself in flowers. Thus flowers are seduction, discourse, a lengthy abandon. Once hard and salty, he is now made completely of flowers, and when he speaks flowers fall from the must of his mouth, and from between his teeth, for he has eaten the flowers I have offered, and has forgotten he has ever been human. I will ruin him with these flowers.

I dreamed of him long ago. And now I offer him flowers.

The Virgin Formica

"Really?"

"When?"

"How long?"

"And with whom?"

"And — by the way — why?"

The answer: back then, we just behaved badly.

But are you still a good person if you've done some "bad" things?

And how do you evaluate you who are now in relation to who you were then, if change is, yes, permanence?

In those days we were stars, shiny as new dimes on the virgin formica, fucking in a bank after hours under merciful Levolors, our no-moon, void-of-course moods barely anticipating history's mighty sea-change in retrograde.

We burst forth in daylight, as living spirits, and the place of our hearts' desires was among the lands of the living forever. We celebrated even Ember Day with vigils, ritual sacrifices, our flats resplendent with the colors of our lady butchers, while a plague of snakes raged in banality on the great maternal estates.

But then things went, as our great comedian said, from back strap to liverwurst, fast forward through time in a sad, comic pantomime of mongoloidism, in dreams of screen doors slamming, in the crash and burn of anticipation, into pools of quietude, until the only outlets for our imperfections were creative collusions with menstruation. We became obsessed with suspension and quirky alternatives to Saturn's stranglehold on our fates. Like pious monks at the Chinese gates we waited, hands folded, penniless in the depths of our memories of cigarette roses.

Then, one by one, we were reduced in our numbers, slipping into absence like sleepwalkers, like gnats among pleasure seekers. We'd known Nature had kept something hidden from us — maybe everything — but Nature had always seemed so quaint, so violable. Who could forget the wide, calm bay, the brisk night breakers, and homely Queen Pia of Serbia, presiding over the competition for the prettiest hands in France? Petrus the Lycanthrope with his scented beard at the opening night orgy of the Carnival and Plague? Rickety kitchens turned into impromptu nightclubs? The sweet apple party sausages we consumed with so much gusto among the sanctimoniously stricken, and then the pleasure of being forgiven? The simple picture postcards of antique toilet water bottles that swept us back to the shores of reality? When those things vanished, or were taken from us, I simply retreated into memories.

Now, when I'm drunk or high, I go into the toilet and close my eyes and there's a whole other world on the other side of the wall, a world of light from another place, and crazed as a satyr with the purity of that light I barrel again into dawn's wet hedges with the power of a thousand spirochetes, soothed by the coolness across the moisture at the small of my back, to flutter up a rotunda on the wave of ambience I once created with my purse.

And the things I hear that give me pleasure are another measure of all that's changed. Once I loved a sequence of shrieks emanating from a poisonous mouth, protestations ad infinitum, the sad, strange, syrupy strains of the "Song of the Voiding of Bones." Otherwordly sounds, they brought me closer to the probity of nightmare.

Now it's the sound of a knife in a mayonnaise jar on a summer night in the country as we sit down at a table under a bug light to play a board game.

Images of contemplation have changed as well. Gone are the photogravure views of prostitutes and newspaper photos of slain society ladies.

Now it's the apricot-colored late afternoon sun on snow that reveals the Mystery.

But does the Mystery still pertain to me?

Can it realign my needs?

Reconfigure lost pleasure?

And then . . .

what?

Nothing?

"Tourist in a Phantom America"
— a five-minute event

for Jill Rappaport

** Introduction: "Infection in the Sentence": an intricately
      choreographed tap dance for seventy-five male
      dancers in Batman masks to the tune of "Yellow Rose of
      Texas," which works to inflame the fabric of a text
      composed and spoken by William Shatner

      occurring simultaneously with:

** flow charts of narrative dream structures mapped out within the
      framework of cell regeneration and neutrino splicing,
      flashing at 1.5 second intervals on three screens suspended
      from the ceiling

      overlaid with:

** the background vocals of Stevie Wonder's "Signed, Sealed,
      Delivered," randomly percolated and regrouped fractally

      followed by:

** "Ritual and Result in the Spanish Radio Broadcasts of the 1990
      World Series by Juan Marichal," a bilingual text delivered
      sotto voce by the current crop of Victoria's Secret models
      over the first twelve bars of "I Want You To Want
      Me" by Cheap Trick (live version, Budokan)

      followed by:

** "Simone de Beauvoir Offers Me a Tampon" — a *tableau*
      vivant featuring Helen Vendler as de Beauvoir and Mick

Jagger as "me" and played in a way that suggests the onset
of a psychological adjustment

followed by:

** two video monitors playing taped interviews of subway
   commuters who took part in a 1982 Rutgers University
   project wherein the phrase "stinking badges" and every "yo!"
   spoken in the first "Rocky" movie were looped to repeat over
   the opening notes of John Coltrane's "A Love Supreme" for
   two weeks on Q trains traveling between DeKalb Avenue and
   34th Street, the purpose of which was to reveal the implied/
   denied armatures of Freudian signifiers so obvious they
   constituted assaults on every orifice

flowing into:

** "Moments of Being, Moments of Non-Being," an address by
   Clint Eastwood, with special material written by William
   Shatner and spoken by Shatner, wherein the direction of
   all previous presentations as a system of active agents
   possessing nonessential cores of identity is revealed as being
   previously overdetermined

and concluding with:

** "The World as Wound," a *cante jondo* with lyrics by Maya
   Angelou and music by Sting, and featuring spoken-word
   interludes by William Shatner (with additional special
   material written by William Shatner)

Begin Transition

The way the sunrise looks this morning is strange —
like it's coming from a different direction.
But it's beautiful too,
like how mornings on other planets in sci-fi movies
are beautiful, with two suns or three moons.
Yesterday the sign on the construction site
by the podiatrist's office said
"Begin transition."
And so, when I got home,
I exfoliated my foot:
long, luminous rivulets of skin,
papery and apricot-colored.

I've been in a cast since August.
I haven't walked on two feet for thirteen weeks.
My leg has atrophied,
is markedly shorter than the other,
while my arms and shoulders are incredibly muscular,
from constant use of a walker.
Vertical extension
is a singular exclusion,
replaced by the flawlessness of tedium.
But within that tedium hides another kind of life:
like when I'm sitting at the kitchen table
and I turn away from the window,
and the flights of birds are reflected
in the shiny surface of formica,
and a woman passing by outside
smells like the fragrant breath of a laundry vent
from a red brick apartment building
that I passed one long ago Chicago October
when the orderly cleanliness of that scent
was merely a reminder

of an anxious evening's lack of comfort:
the dark dirty kitchen,
the stained slop sink,
the oblique metal fittings
of glossolalia:
of silver/crack/intrude,
of an angry person's wisdom —
death wish, fleshy kingdom —
a parasite's suicide
which is really just a vast appetite for life.
Oh, you who were my poverty.
But the fetters of forgetfulness
are temporary
and speak of another kind of purity,
maybe Lucifer's purity
      (it must be an allegory
        of the memory
         of drunkards joining hands),
of prudence,
beauty,
humility,
the romantic exuberance
of goo.

What am I doing?
This isn't memory,
but the illusion
of remembering:
a new cuteness
relating to history
and the everyday,
like the popularity
of Rachael Ray.
Fuck that chipmunk.
The real need right now
is to dust/sweep/mop,
toss away all nonsense,

take down those cardboard boxes,
replace them with expensive plastic boxes,
and find or design a system of efficient, color-coded filing.
And, most of all, pick my skin up off the floor,
start sending out submissions,
begin the aforementioned transition,
because the sunrise this morning is strange
like it's coming from another direction.

What You Were Dreaming Of

The blue cold?
the static crackle?
the reciting of the bones of the feet?

The trickle of water
in the radiator
and the gunpowder green
tea?

A dull Dixon Ticonderoga?

A Laurel and Hardy movie?

The Thanksgiving Day parade?

The sparkling army
of pre-lit trees?

The glimmering corsets
in midair
and huge icy oaks
shining in the night?

The bubble that bruises
the side of the tube?

The scent of the Orient
that opens the pores?

Is that what you were dreaming of?
Finest hardwoods and herbs?
simple huts and wikkiups?

Half a battlement column
occluded by skyscrapers?
insolent suburbanity
amused by birch brooches?

Big hips and a sloppy grin
are never embarrassed
to take up space.

The messy charisma
of a trust fund foster child
parodies an earlier self.

Which bird-god
can save us now?
which blood-soaked idealist
stumbling through a nightmare?

Who is the mouse savior?
the cockroach liaison?

An eyelash on the page
plays the witness game
against the permanence
of paper,

and the ones about to shoot
stand in the shadow
of the hill,
while the ones about to die
are blindfolded
wearing white
and stand on the hill
in sunlight,

arms outstretched
as if about to fly.

The heavy motion-weight
of staves
the palm-wine
hosannahs
hammer out
the ordinary

and five years later
you'll see yourself
as others saw you:

as tesserae
as Clackamas
as ubiquitous
liquids
in Paris gutters.

Now, turn over the cards.

Pray for swords.

On the Occasion of Turning Forty at the Age of Forty-Two

I maintain,
for the sake of argument,
that happiness occurs
in trouble and astonishment,
in the beauty that accrues
from just showing up,
the movement from "he loves me" to
"he loves me not,"
the length and breadth
of an Abyssinian head,
the bald, brilliant sun
of New Brunswick,
docile camels,
a happy new year.
Some amusing, intricate rules
come later,
and I am the instigator
in those matters,
having the power
to reincarnate
without the inconvenience
of dying.

By the Waters Off Brooklyn

And so, on to other, more curious loves:
beautiful and cruel Johnny Templar,
rent boy of summer, living in a trailer
by the waters off Brooklyn.
Along the peripheries of dawn's moorings
we ran barking,
tugged into further reluctant adjustments
by bright Lucifer
and the daytime moon.
In the afternoon we napped in half-light,
waking and groaning with a mild foreboding,
a feeling akin to "agog."
By evening there was the crescendo
of air conditioners dripping
as we were again bedding
in the back of a van
parked in the lot
of the Mart of the Wall,
covered in the whiz of cheese.
Afterwards we strutted, shamelessly wanking,
onto a carnival midway,
ran naked into a Rorschach test,
and poked even dainty people.
Yet even as morality abandoned me
I remained girlish and strange,
at one with Destiny
though betrayed by Fate,
bolstered by the childhood dream
in which Jesus told me
that I had the aura of genius.
Too bad I don't believe in Jesus.

The few druids who knew how to use letters
could spell out a message
only initiates could interpret.
On the surface, it seemed to be about a battle of trees.
but really it was the secret of a painful ritual
to restore innocence.
But the goal nowadays
is not the cessation of pain
but the living inside of it,
to glean what it seeks to teach.
But that's easy for me to say;
I'm already looking for a new way
out of no way,
ready to trade sex for a chance
to be a child again.
What's the purpose of birth, anyway?

But, honey, understand that I represent
neither vulgar human congress nor tyranny.
The pin I stuck into my skull for penance
changed me
first, into a bird,
then a ring swallowed by a fish,
and finally a flying horse that lived next door.
Can evil be holy, too?
That answer the Kitty of Now should know.
But these my burdens are not easily overcome
by small stones and slingshots.
The three minutes' happiness I was promised
was just a visitor to my ken.
And so, alone of my sex among Templars,
I set out to decipher the secrets of my refrigerator:
five spicy brown mustards meant travel, change, variety;
six pico de gallos, home, service, family;
seven ketchups, spirituality, analysis, and knowlege.
I negotiated those ideas slowly,
like a juggler with no sense of rhythm,

or that sad clown with a cigarette in his mouth:
my dad.
He had a bod like a beat up car with
"I'm Free, Take Me"
taped to the trunk.
"Sometimes the space provided by Jesus,"
 he said on his deathbed,
 "is sinfully insufficient.
  Still, there's always enough space
  to sign your name."
And that's what I always say.
Or, to put it another way:
fish once walked on dry land,
and ancient whales had ankles.
Their fossils came from Pakistan.

Sadly, greatness escapes me.
I'm lucky to have two rooms and a bathroom,
to be the hunchback's brother's replacement.
These days, the best part of waking up
is if I don't throw up,
and my special prayer for you,
which I sincerely hope you'll use, is
"Please God, don't let me puke."
I was once curt and furtive, yet festive, too.
Then came the crisis that obliterated my crinoline,
and the hooligan who ruined me —
beautiful and cruel Johnny Templar.
We hold these truths to be dope tropes:
that experience is its own reward,
and punishment.
So let's breakfast in silence on the frontage road,
with the thunder above and the lava below.
There, west of center,
the earth shall immure us in its metals.
Every day will be a matinee
from which we'll emerge surprised

that there's still such a thing as light.
The swinging screen door of spiritual purity,
the small town ice cream parlor awning of otherworldly beauty —
there is only one moment, and this is it.
Everything depends on the deep end.

I'm Not Sorry

for Jeff Swimmer

"I'm sorry," he said,
"but cunts really do smell like tuna."

"Oh yeah?" I said.
"Well dicks smell like Clorox,
  the actual dick I mean,
  and that area between the dick and the balls
  smells like that plastic stuff they sell way west on Canal Street
  by the Holland Tunnel,
  but the balls themselves are more like
  if a shoebox from the 1940s could sweat,
  and then if you go back farther back toward the asshole
  it's like rancid talcum powder,
  specifically Gold Bond Medicated Powder,
  and you might think that the asshole smells like shit,
  and of course it does,
  but there's this under smell,
  kinda like the cheese on French Onion Soup
  if it's been standing for a coupla hours,
  but not the French Onion Soup you get here —
  the real kind,
  ya know,
  from *France*."

Song of Myself

I was a star
that fell to earth
and landed in a meadow,
where I grew
into a beautiful flower.
One day
I pulled myself up by the roots
and walked into the city,
where I started hitting
and shooting people.
This is the Song of Myself.
Now die, you fuckers.

Acknowledgments

Some of these poems have appeared in the magazines *New American Writing, OCHO 14, lungfull!, Lit 12, Hanging Loose, lingo 8, Brooklyn Rail, Poetry Project Newsletter, Hjir* (Netherlands), *Tears in the Fence* (UK), *Purple* (France), *Barfout!* (Japan) and *Van Gogh's Ear* (France); in the anthologies *Heights of the Marvelous* (St. Martin's Press, Todd Colby, editor), *Outlaw Bible of American Poetry* (Thunder's Mouth Press, Alan Kaufman, editor), *The Second Word Thursdays Anthology* (Bright Hill Press, Bertha Rogers, editor-in-chief) and *The Portable Boog Reader* (Boog Literature, David Kirschenbaum, editor); and on the websites *respiro, big bridge, theeastvillage* and *rattapallax POeP!.* Many thanks to the editors and publishers, and sincere apologies if I've inadvertently forgotten anyone.

"Never Lose Your Sense of Wonder" was written for a reading at the Institute of Contemporary Art/University of Pennsylvania (thanks to Tom Devaney).

"Madame Bowery," with drawings by David Borchart, appeared in *Hanging Loose* 83 and in Romanian translation (without drawings) by Paul Doru Mugur on the website www.respiro.org (thanks to Paul and the *respiro* editors).

"Flowers" appeared on t-shirts designed by Junichi Tsunoda (thanks to Yumiko Sato, Ayumi Miyake and Taskashi Hata).

The poems "Lonely Tylenol," "By the Waters Off Brooklyn," and "Madame Bowery" appeared in the book *Lonely Tylenol*, in collaboration with David Humphrey, published by Flying Horse Editions/University of Central Florida, 2004 (thanks to David Humphrey and Ryan Burkhardt).

The poems "Lou Reed's New York," "Laid," "At Princess Olga's," "Stupid University Job," "Brenda Coultas's Coat" and "Retarded Aerosmith World" appeared in the chapbook *Vertigo Seeks Affinities*, published by Belladonna Press, 2006 (thanks to Erica Kaufman, Stacey Szymaczek and Rachel Levitsky).

The poems "For the Time Being" and "Laid" appeared in Romanian translation (as "Deocamdata" and "Laid") in *Scrisul Românesc* and on the site www.revistascrisulromanesc.ro (thanks to Carmen Firan and Paul Doru Mugur).

Many thanks to the New York Foundation for the Arts, the MacDowell Colony, Hawthornden Castle and Fundación Valparaíso for the fellowships which provided me with much-needed time and encouragement during the writing and completion of this book.

Many thanks, once again, to Donna Brook, Bob Hershon, Marie Carter, Mark Pawlak and Dick Lourie. Extra special thanks to Donna for extreme editing.